Edited by Brooke Vitale

ISBN: 978-1-953384-29-4 (e-book)

ISBN: 978-1-953384-28-7 (paperback)

ISBN: 978-1-953384-21-8 (hardcover)

Library of Congress Control Number: 2022917244

First edition 2023
Printed in China

Published by Eternal Tree Books LLC
East Brunswick, NJ
www.eternaltreebooks.com

Dedicated to my Maa, and to all the wonderful parents who are the first gurus of their children. ——BA

To Devi - my eternal mother, Sadhguru and my parents who brought the experience of this book alive within me. ——SA

Maa is the most amazing human
I know.

She teaches me about being kind to others and
about becoming a good human being.
But even without her words, I am reminded of her messages.

Each morning,
Maa's saree speaks to me.
In it, I see the world.
I see who I can be.

Thoughts of goodness, love, hope, and peace flow from it,
reminding me of the lessons she's shared.
What she's said once, her sarees tell me time and again.

In Maa's blue saree, I see my home:
the limitless blue sky.
"Sky," she tells me, "is the home for all.
It protects us with goodness so vast."

I bow to this blue to receive its goodness—
To my Maa and the sky.

Her green saree shades me,
like a tree soaked in immense love.

“Trees,” she tells me, “give us air to breathe,
and leaves that can help us heal.”

I see Maa bowing to the trees
and know that they are friends
who give us life.

Together we sow more seeds—
seeds of love,
this time—protecting the trees
for the generations to come.

Maa's saree holds the greenish blue tides of the sea.

She tells me about the tides—that they will come and go,
that they will wash away what you make with sand.
"Don't be disheartened," Maa says, "as this is what life is about.
The world is always changing.
Each day will bring an empty canvas,
just like the washed away sand.
Each day, you will have to make something new and better."

"It is in your hands how you craft your life.
The empty canvas will empower you.
This power is Shiva,
the power of the creative void.
Celebrate this possibility, of becoming and creating."

I think of Maa's bluish green saree when I paint on blank sheets— to draw on the floor, on the walls, on any empty space I see.

I wonder if that is the power of Shiva, too—the power of emptiness that pulls me to create something from nothing.

In Maa's vibrant red saree, I see Devi, the goddess of power.
Maa tells me not to fear unjust things, that it is Devi who destroys our fear.

So pure, so strong, Maa stands against all that would push her down.
I watch the swish of her red saree and I long to be determined like Maa.
She is like the goddess of power.

In Maa's yellow saree, I see the rising sun.
"Yellow is the color of a stable and happy mind," Maa tells me.
"A mind like that of Krishna.
Wherever you go, whatever you do,
carry peace and calm with you.
Anger and frustration will only keep you from being the best you can be."
When Maa dresses me in yellow,
I try to be the best I can be.
I try to be like her:
never bothered, angry, or frustrated.
Like Krishna, Maa finds solutions with a happy smile.
I let the peace of her yellow wash over me,
and try to do the same.

Maa's orange saree reminds me of the tales she tells of yogis—
of the way they meditate, dressed in orange.

"Orange," she tells me, "is the color of realizing, knowing, and connecting.
It is the color of moving beyond our personal wants.
When you close your eyes and meditate, you connect with everything around you.
You can feel the pain and happiness of others.
To be in bliss is to become one with all that's around."

I see Maa's saree, and I wonder if we are all connected.

Like Maa, I also sit and close my eyes.

I try to connect as she does—

To feel happy when someone smiles, and to know when they are sad.

What a beautiful world it will be if we all cared for the feelings of everyone around.

In Maa's white saree I see Sarasvati,
the goddess of wisdom who shines like the Moon
She sits on a white lotus and plays the veena.

"Books are where we find her blessings," says Maa.
"So joyful and motherly she looks,
singing a lullaby full of wisdom—
inspiring us to speak kind and truthful words."

I listen, pressed against Maa's white saree as she reads inspiring books to me.
Like the goddess, she brings the light of knowledge to me.

In her black saree,
Maa looks bold, like thundering clouds.
Soaked in the feelings of everyone around,
she listens to me, to my problems and questions
She sits, ready to receive all that I bring,
whether it is love, questions, or tantrums.

She takes away my problems like water evaporating from the sea,
only to bring the rain of new beginning.
Her embrace allows me to clear my head,
to see things as they are.

In her brown saree, I see the Earth—
a leaf born in the lap of soil,
from a seed that finds its home in the ground.
The mother and the Earth,
both give us birth,
for they make us who we are and what we think.
We become what we eat, what we listen to, and who we love.
I bow in thanks to Maa and the Earth.

Today she wears a saree with so many colors.
“Many is the beauty of life,” says Maa.

"Many plants, many animals, many seasons,
many stars, many rivers, many mountains,
many feelings, many emotions, many problems, many solutions.
Embrace all colors of life, for life is full of the many."

Seeing Maa's many colors remind me to enjoy life to the fullest—
to take in the many and the beauty of difference.
I play different games, draw different pictures,
eat different fruits, smell different flowers, befriend different people.

I am not the same as others, and they are not the same as me. And that is okay.

I know that no matter what the color of her saree,
Maa is watching me.

We see in each other her messages
of becoming a good human being,
of my love for her and hers for me,
of defining her and of finding me.

AUTHOR'S NOTE

A mother, in all cultures, is considered extremely precious. In Hinduism, we call our parents *Bhagavan*—the Divine. They are the ones who make us who we are. From the time we are born, our parents nurture us, protect us, train us, and give us good values. They become teachers or friends, depending on our age. This book is a tribute to all parents, and especially mothers, around the world.

This is a story of a mother who inspires her son to become a better human being. The son loves the mother and her sarees. He links the teachings of his mother to her sarees. What his mother teaches him, her sarees reinforce, taking the reader on a journey of not only understanding the values of Hinduism, but of also feeling the respect a young son has for his mother.

In the Indian tradition, children are given a universal identity before any formal education. They are first initiated into *aham brahmasmi* (I am because of everything, and I am everything). I was inspired to write this book by my relationship with my mother who sowed the seeds of this identity in me. Just like any other child, I would look up to her for everything from food to clothes to bath to sleep. As a toddler, if I hurt myself while playing, the first thing I would do would be to look for my mother. I would simply hug her and go back to play. Just her presence meant a lot to me. Gradually, my problems and needs started to evolve. I had more and more questions about what I saw, experienced, felt, or heard. From being sad after breaking a toy to fearing darkness, her words always inspired me to find the solution within. Her messages were aimed to make me sensitive towards my surroundings, people, and Nature. She would pick either a color, or a deity, or something happening in Nature to help me relate to things I'd seen. The first thing that comes to my mind when I think about my mother is her sarees. Sarees have adorned Indian women for thousands of years—women who have inspired and shaped our generations. I have grown up seeing my mother enjoy wearing sarees, and it is something I identify her with. That's why I chose the saree as a vehicle for sharing what my mother told me while growing up. These conversations between my mother and me, will tell you about what different colors mean to me, what is their cultural significance to me, and how they continue to inspire me.

For instance, blue reminds me of the inspirational Bhagavan Rama who is depicted with blue skin. Blue shows his sky-like, limitless compassion. In Sanskrit texts, sky is also compared to a father, and Sri Rama was a fatherly king who cared for his people. Equivalence between a father and the sky is also seen in the word Ju-piter, which is from the Sanskrit root words ***Dyau*** for 'sky' and ***Pitar*** for 'father.' Also, the word father—***Pater*** in Greek—has the Sanskrit verb ***Pa***, meaning, to protect. Similarly, Sanskrit texts also draw parallels between the Earth and a mother. Brown color represents soil—the Earth. It is like our mother who nurtures us and gives us food. Like our moms make us who we are, different foods—depending on their yogic qualities: ***Sattva, Rajas***, and ***Tamas***—also have a deep impact on our mental and physical well-being. Many ***Sattvic*** foods, like most fruits and vegetables given by the Earth, can really help us become calmer and reduce our need for long hours of sleep. Foods rich in the other two qualities—plant based or not—may not be the best for consumption, especially if one wants to gain spiritually from yogic practices. That is why I mentioned in the story "we become what we eat."

I have written many such messages of virtues, well-being, peace, and respect in this story with the hope of inspiring children to grow into thankful, graceful, compassionate, and responsible citizens. I hope sons respect their wonderful moms even more and become kind men who respect women in all walks of life. It starts with the realization: "Maa is the most amazing human I know."

GLOSSARY

Devi Refers to the divine feminine deities of Hinduism like Goddess Durga, Lakshmi, and Sarasvati. This term is also used after a lady's name to show respect. It means one who is glorious and splendid. In the story it is used to refer to Goddess Durga.

Krishna A very popular Hindu deity worshipped in different forms—as a baby, as a teenage boy, and as a statesman and guru. His life has timeless and profound messages that continue to inspire families even today. It is common for young children to dress like Him on his birthday, popularly known as Janmashtami.

Maa Mother.

Sarasvati Hindu goddess of wisdom, music, arts, and knowledge. She represents the peaceful mind of a seeker who strives to gain knowledge and eventually, bliss. This name also refers to the ancient river in northwest India which holds high importance in the evolution of the Indian civilization. Just the way the mighty river flowed once, the image of Sarasvati symbolizes a peaceful river of knowledge that inspires students and teachers of today.

Saree One of the most famous attires for women, popular in the Indian subcontinent since ancient times. Wearing unstitched fabric like the saree has many subtle health benefits in the system of yoga. Experts also talk about the benefits of draping the saree the way it is usually done and the importance of wearing organic cotton or silk sarees.

Shiva One of the most prominent Hindu deities. Symbolizes the concept of the creative void—nothingness, where all that exists comes from and goes back to. Life needs constant change, evolution, transformation, and regeneration. This power or consciousness is Shiva.

Veena Musical instrument representing divine music and harmony, held by Goddess Sarasvati. Famous since the Vedic times and very hard to master. It is known to express human emotions and its music is therapeutic.

Yogi A person who realizes the true nature of life by doing yogic practices and meditation. Yoga means union of the mind and the body and also union with all beings and Nature. Yogi is a person who is united with all that is around.